I0493358

MONEY
IN YOUR POCKET
How to Generate a Second
Income in Just 4 Hours a Week

Paul E Coan

All rights reserved. No part of this publication may be reproduced, distributed, or transmitted in any form or by any means, including photocopying, recording, or other electronic or mechanical methods, without the prior written permission of the publisher, except in the case of a brief quotations embodied in critical reviews and certain other noncommercial uses permitted by copyright law. For permission request, write to the publisher at publisher@paulcoan.com.

No patent liability is assumed with respect to the use of the information contained herein. Although every precaution has been take in the preparation of this publication, the publisher and author assume no responsibility for errors or omissions. Neither is any liability assumed for damages resulting from the use of information contained herein.

Copyright © 2014 Paul Coan

All rights reserved.

ISBN:1496036018
ISBN-978-1496036018

DEDICATION

To those who know, hard work pays, but wants to work smarter.

Free Accompanying Course

It's practically universal to want to increase your income. Regardless of how much money someone has, they would still like to make more. That is why in an effort to take this book beyond its pages, we have created a multi-part course that extends the ideas in this book. You will receive a 29 page book, worksheets and PowerPoint presentation entitled "Passive Profits: Do It Once and Profit Forever" to help you achieve that universal income goal.

Sign up for free at http://www.paulcoan.com/passive-profits (if you are using a standard kindle you may want to do this from your computer). And don't worry; we have much better things to do with our time than share your email address with spammers.

Sign Up At: http://www.paulcoan.com/passive-profits

CONTENTS

ACKNOWLEDGMENTS

A project such as this is seldom due to the efforts of the author alone. Many people assisted me in one way or another with the preparation of this book. Without the interest and suggestions offered by a supportive group of individuals, Money in Your Pocket would have never been compiled for print. I am deeply indebted to my devoted wife, Ann, for her technical and creative help, I surely could not have produced this work without her support and assistance.

In addition, I extend my sincere appreciation to those great people who are implementing one or more of these ideas and where not afraid to share their story. My best wishes for you and your family in pursuing your dreams.

CHAPTER 1

MAKE MONEY AT THE FARMER'S MARKET

Bringing in extra money to bump up your bottom line requires putting your creativity to work. If you can open your mind wide to the possibilities that might exist in your backyard or even within your skillset, you'll be amazed at the enjoyable and unexpected ways you can make money.

A pathway to more green that you may not have thought about is becoming an active participant in your local farmer's markets. This guide will help you realize the possibilities that farmer's markets can bring in terms of financial success.

What to Look for During Your Next Farmer's Market Foray.

This weekend, attend your farmer's market. Instead of just running through to pick up produce for the week, take your time examining what you see and what's going on there. Observe.

What are people selling? Of course, the standard fruits and vegetables are available. But what else? Maybe there are freshly-cut herbs, pretty baskets of assorted soaps, and even some small hand-crafted tools for the kitchen, like whisks or cleaning brushes. You might want to jot down the array of products available for sale.

Notice how vendors are displaying their products. This one is particularly important because it lends some info about what type of overhead costs you may generate to display your own wares and products.

Are they simply laid out on a fold-out table? Is there a decorative table cloth? How are the items for sale packaged? Are fresh herbs tied with decorative ribbon, simply spread out so people can pick up how much they want, or banded with a rubber band? Is there package wrapping to consider?

Look for simple, no-frills, yet attractive ways that products are displayed. Which product displays attract you? Make notes.

Ask yourself, "What's missing?" Now that you have a good idea of what's for sale, ponder what types of products you and others might like to purchase from the farmer's market.

Look for signs or pamphlets about who's in charge. Usually, there's someone you can talk to about how to become involved in the farmer's market. If there's a phone number or name of the organizers posted, write it down. It may be the local town's business association or chamber of commerce. Get down that info so you can call them later with your questions.

This information may also be found in the newspaper article that advertises the market.

WHAT COULD YOU MAKE TO SELL AT THE FARMER'S MARKETS?

When you get home, take a look at things you're good at and what you do that earns kudos from others. Your next income stream might also flow from something you love to do.

What are you good at? Maybe you love to try different soup recipes. Why not buy up some quart-size Mason jars and sell your freshly-made and jarred soups at the farmer's market?

When do you get compliments from others? If people rave over your five-ingredient homemade bread, maybe it's time to start a cottage industry baking and selling loaves of it.

Perhaps your garden isn't all that large but you love to get fresh produce and make your own salsas and jellies. With a case or two of pint-sized wide mouthed jars, you'd be all set for next week's market. Stick with simple, natural ingredients to make things easy for you. Plus, customers love the idea of buying something that's homemade.

What do you love to do? Of course, you can sell fruits and vegetable from your own garden, and maybe even sell small plants, like a strawberry pot already planted with strawberry plants or an herb pot full of growing herb plants for kitchens.

Perhaps you think there's nothing more fun than making homemade soaps and tying them up in stacks of two or three to give to friends   for birthdays and holiday gifts. You love seeing all the pretty colors and smelling all the fragrances and the idea of others using soaps you made yourself. Plus, it's easy and fun to do on a Sunday afternoon.

INSPIRING IDEAS FOR FARMER'S MARKET PROFIT

Just to get your creative juices flowing, consider some of these suggestions for what you could sell at the farmer's market. Bringing in more cash can be an enjoyable process.

Wood-crafted items. Maybe your grandpa taught you how to make small carvings from wood. You like to do it but you never know what to do with all the left-over creations. Selling them at the farmer's market is your answer.

Knitted, crocheted, or sewn items. Many people love the idea of given a hand-crafted gift to others or even treating themselves to something extravagant from time to time.

Consider making washcloths, dishcloths, dishtowels, potholders, hats, purses, change purses, small gift bags, water bottle carriers, grocery store totes, baby blankets, booties, and sweaters, coasters, placemats, cell phone socks, or an item you create.

Baked foods. Who doesn't love a fresh-baked treat to take home with them or present as a special gift to someone? Think about small wrapped clusters of cookies or candies, baked cakes, muffins, cinnamon rolls, and the like. If your forte is making such goodies, this could be the way to go.

Jarred gifts. If you think you lack skills in hand-crafting hobbies and you're not much of a baker, why not consider buying some Mason jars and layering ingredients for cookies, bars, bean soups, or even cocoa mixes into the jar? If you don't already have recipes for such items; look on the internet to find them. Tailor the recipe to make it your own.

Print up a decorative label and instructions on how to mix up or cook the food and tie a decorative square or round of fabric over the top of the jar. Voila! You've got an interesting, enticing, and money-making product to sell.

IT'S ALL ABOUT THE PRESENTATION

After you decide on what you're willing to make to sell at farmer's markets, decide how you can attractively display and present your items to entice prospective customers to your table at the market.

How can you make your table pretty? Maybe all you'll need is a one-color plastic tablecloth.

Think of color themes. Limit color selections on your table and packaging to no more than three to avoid looking "too busy."

Consider how you'll package your product. If it's fresh herbs, you   may not need much but some light rubber bands and big baskets to display your bunched sprigs. If you're selling homemade noodles using your grandma's recipe, how will you inexpensively package them to look appetizing?

Include typed-up directions for anything that requires the

customer to blend, mix, or put together a food item. Don't forget to put your contact information somewhere on the product.

FINAL STEPS TO BECOME A FARMER'S MARKET VENDOR

Contact the organizers of the market by phone or in person when you go to the farmer's market. Tell them you have a product you'd like to sell.

Ask if you're required to have a business license to sell your products at the market. Find out where you can apply for and obtain such a license.

Tell the organizers about what you plan to sell and listen to any feedback they offer. Although they might not restrict you from selling your fresh herbs from your backyard herb garden, they may tell you they already have two regular vendors who sell them.

Don't be concerned if you're told, "We've never sold that before." Bringing fresh ideas can be a welcome addition for the market and make you some nice cash at the same time.

Consider it an adventure to boost your income by trying your hand at the local farmer's market. Wouldn't it be great to have an additional income stream to pad your bank account?

CHAPTER 2

PUBLIC SPEAKING

If you're looking for a way to significantly boost your income, public speaking might be the answer. Speaking fees of $40,000 or more aren't uncommon. The average professional speaker makes approximately $6,000 per speech!

It might seem far-fetched if you've never given a paid speech, but it's easier than you think.

There are a variety of ways to earn a lot of money for your time, but most will fall into one of two broad categories:

Doing something that most others can't. These are the things with a high barrier to entry. This would include activities like playing professional sports or becoming a brain surgeon. It's not possible to simply start doing these things and expect to start earning a paycheck tomorrow.

Doing things that others don't want to do. Dealing with nuclear waste or living on an oil rig 100 miles out in the middle of nowhere would qualify here.

Public speaking falls into the latter category. Not many people enjoy public speaking, which is part of the reason professional speakers are paid so well.

Follow these tips to come up with a great speech and join

the ranks of well-paid speakers:

Learn how to give a good speech! Perhaps the best solution to this step is joining Toastmasters International. They can have 20+ chapters in just one medium sized city. The cost is minimal. Most chapters meet about 4 times per month, though some meet more and some less.

You have the opportunity to speak at every meeting, and the members take turns leading the meetings. You receive immediate feedback and speeches are recorded.

Consider joining multiple chapters to get more practice! Chapters meet on a variety of days at a variety of times. There's bound to be a day and time that work for you.

There are also additional opportunities for learning other skills and networking with business leaders in your community.

Figure out what you're going to talk about. There are several different types of public speakers:

Informational. These speakers educate and teach others about a specialized topic. It might be providing information about a piece of software or teaching something about bass fishing. Maybe it's a speech about Buddhism or an exciting African safari.

Inspirational/motivational. Often these speakers relate stories of   hardship, overcoming adversity, or achieving great things.

Humorous. Everyone likes to laugh.

It's important to figure out what your exact topic is going to be. What do you know that could be valuable to others? What fascinating things have you done or experienced? Are you great at making people laugh? Brainstorm a few ideas and share them with your fellow Toastmasters.

Create your speech. Think about how long you want your talk to be. Are you interested in talking for an entire day? A professional speech can be as short as 30 minutes. A good plan might be to create a 2-hour speech and a shorter version of 30 minutes.

Practice with your Toastmasters group. Once you have your speech written and practiced several times, try it out on your new group of friends. You'll receive tons of expert feedback. Record your speech so you can critique yourself later and see your progress over time.

Keep improving and practicing. Take the constructive criticism to heart and keep improving your speech. When you've improved it, practice again with your Toastmasters group.

MARKETING YOURSELF

Now that you have a great speech, it's time to find an audience. While many people, like Olympic medal winners and famous politicians, can start at the top of the pay scale, you might have to start closer to the bottom and work your way up.

There are many ways to find some work:

Consider giving a free speech. Many speakers started out giving free speeches. Consider what groups would like to hear your information and contact them. After one or two free speeches, you can probably start getting paid. It's very common to find your first client from your audience. There are plenty of free opportunities to speak if you just ask.

Sign up with a speaker's bureau. These companies are like a clearinghouse for public speakers. Those that wish to hire a speaker can peruse the listings and pick out a speaker. The speaking bureau will normally take a cut of your fee, but they will also normally handle the logistics, scheduling, and collecting your fee.

Set up your own website. Put short video clips of your speech online. Let people see what you have to offer. Really take the time to put your best foot forward. Take advantage of YouTube, too.

Make it easy to connect with you. At the very least, have your phone and email on the front of your web page.

Learn how to fully utilize social media. Use every tool at your disposal.

Create a "speaking brief." This is similar to a resume. It should include a good photo, a paragraph mentioning your speech topics, your background, speaking experience, references, links to videos of your speeches, and your contact info.

Be seen. Be everywhere you can be. Get up on the stage at every opportunity. Comment on relevant blogs, write a guest post for a website, go to events, and meet as many people as possible. People need to know you and what you have to offer.

Keep pushing. After your early speeches are behind you, you might be charging $2,500. It could be $10,000 in a year. The key is to continue improving and asking for more money as you get more experience. Many times, the only difference between the $2,500 speaker and the $25,000 speaker is that the latter simply asks for more money.

Build relationships. Along the way you'll meet many people. Stay in regular contact. Make friends with these people. Word-of-mouth is always the best way to find new speaking engagements.

Even if you've never given a speech, you can become a professional speaker and do so successfully on a part-time basis. Just as you don't have to be the best auto mechanic to make a living, you don't have to be the world's greater public speaker either.

Take the time to learn to speak well. It doesn't take long. Very few people do public speaking on a regular basis, so you can be better than 99% of the general population very quickly.

Make a great speech, practice, and get out there. Market like your life depends on it. Many groups are constantly looking for good content. Let them know about yours!

You might even decide to quit your day job!

CHAPTER 3

THE KEYS TO SUCCESSFUL MOONLIGHTING

A second source of income is always welcome.

Or maybe you have dreams of escaping your regular job and want to start your own business. Well, it would be great to have that business going reasonably well before you quit the first job.

For your best results, keep these ideas in mind as you create that second income:

Brainstorm. Consider all the possibilities for your second income. How many hours can you give to it each week? Does it need to be on the weekends only? How much money can you expect to make? How long will it take to start making money?

Come up with a big list and then evaluate all your options.

Value your time. Be smart; it really doesn't make sense to take a part-time job making minimum wage. Anyone can do better than that with a little bit of work and planning.

Even something simple like walking a dog pays around $15 for a half-hour walk. There's no reason to flip burgers for $7.50 an hour. You'd get some exercise and have the opportunity to enjoy the outdoors, too.

Consider your strengths. Whatever you choose to generate your second income should either be something that you're good at or truly love. If you love doing it, you'll learn to be good. Also, if you love it, it won't really seem like work.

Ideally, you'll both love it and be great at it. For example:

If you're an accountant, doing something related to accounting makes sense.

If you love to clean, a house cleaning service might be a great idea.

If you love dogs, you could offer dog walking, training, or grooming services.

Be thrifty. Be careful about spending a lot of money to get started. One of the keys to being successful at your own business is to improve along the way. What if your first attempts don't work out so well? It's important that your early mistakes be inexpensive mistakes.

Be timely. Try to find a way to generate some income quickly. Remember, it's likely to be challenging at first.

You don't want to finally find out that your initial plan won't work after toiling for 3 months. Design a plan that will give feedback quickly. You can then fine-tune your approach and eventually put more long-term plans in place.

Schedule time daily. A tremendous amount can be accomplished with just a couple of hours each day.

Turn off the TV. Work on your side business during your

lunch break. Make phone calls during your commute. Every little bit helps to get your freelancing business going when you're first starting out.

Focus on activities that directly generate income. Avoid getting caught in the trap of staying super busy on the things that don't contribute to your income. Many times, the most important actions are the least enjoyable.

Keep in mind that in many cases, financially successful people simply spend a lot of time doing things that the average person doesn't want to do. Things like cold calling and giving presentations are good examples of this concept.

Protect your first income. Be careful with who you share your plans. If you have a professional position, many employers frown upon having another income. They feel that if you have extra time, you should be spending it on your first job.

If you have a good-paying job, it might take awhile to replace that income.

Be careful about using your company cell phone, computer, copier, and other items that belong to your employer for your new business. Technically it's theft, and while you're unlikely to go to jail, it's entirely possible you could lose your job.

Be persistent. Successful people have typically failed far more times than the average person.

Keep working and improving. If something doesn't work the way you expect, try something else. If you simply change your approach until it works, how can you fail?

Consider all the possible sources of income. What else could you include in your business to make even more money? What are some related services you could offer? Avoid

getting caught in the trap of staying super busy on the things that don't contribute to your income. Many times, the most important actions are the least enjoyable.

Let's Look at an Example

Suppose your current job has you working nights. You decide that you can spend a few hours during the day on your second income.

After making a long list of ideas, you like the idea of starting a dog-walking business. You love dogs, and it's something that has nearly unlimited potential. After all, there are a lot of dogs in any city.

You're also available when most people are at work. It seems perfect. All you need is a phone and a leash, so it's easy and inexpensive.

How will you find clients?

You might get started by going to the local dog park and talking to the dog owners

Hand out business cards or give them a simple flyer you made on your computer

Post the offer on Craigslist.org

Hang a flyer in the Laundromat.

Contact the local veterinarians and ask for referrals.

Make a Facebook page.

Consider all the people you know that have dogs and all the people your friends and family know that have dogs

It's easy to see that there are a lot of free and very inexpensive ways to find clients. You can consider spending more money after you start making money.

You might start out walking only 5 dogs Monday through Friday. If you charged $15 for each dog, that would be $375 a week or $1,500 a month.

How hard do you really think it would be to find 5 busy people that need their dog walked around lunchtime every day?

How could you grow this business larger?

You can't walk 100 dogs a day and your time is limited. People don't need their dogs walked 30 minutes after they leave home or 30 minutes before they get home. There's only a small window in the middle of the day that makes sense unless people are on vacation.

You could expand your business by hiring others.

Imagine a team of dog walkers working for you. A lot of people would be happy to earn $10 an hour walking dogs. If they each walked 5 dogs, they could bring in $75 an hour to your business, so that extra $65 goes in your pocket. Do the math; it adds up quickly!

What additional services could you offer that would allow you to generate even more income?

Water the dog owner's plants

Bring in the owner's mail

Feed and give water to the dog

Pick up the droppings in the backyard

Brush the dog

Give the dog a bath

Train the dog

Transport the dog to the vet

You could have a list of these services with a fee schedule and give it to each of your clients.

Not only will it make more money for you when your clients tack on these extra services to their bill, but they'll be grateful for your

fine customer service! You'll be going over and above what other dog walkers might offer them.

As you can see, starting a sideline business that you can grow into something meaningful can be relatively easy and fun!

There's also the possibility to earn a lot more money than you're making now.

Create a plan now for a business you'll really enjoy and get started as soon as possible. You'll be amazed where you end up!

CHAPTER 4

USING A VIRTUAL ASSISTANT TO MARKET YOUR BUSINESS

Trying to conquer the business world alone is tough. We've all wished we had a clone of ourselves to do the busywork that's common in marketing tasks, while we work on other critical tasks.

However, there's an economical solution to this dilemma. It's called the virtual assistant, or V A. **A virtual assistant is a self-employed person who provides technical, administrative, or creative assistance to clients remotely from a home office.**

You can let your VA work through your to-do-list while you focus on the more important or enjoyable tasks. Once you've shown your VA how to upload a mailing list, post ads to Craigslist, or return phone calls, she can keep repeating those tasks as your needs dictate.

A virtual assistant can also be perfect for other marketing tasks, because these tasks tend to be repetitive and lend themselves to step-by-step processes.

ADVANTAGES OF VIRTUAL ASSISTANTS

VS. LOCAL ASSISTANTS

The primary advantages of virtual assistants over local assistants are:

Taxes are simplified. It's much easier to prove your assistant isn't an actual employee if they work remotely.

The costs are usually much less. With some legwork, it's possible to find decent VA's for $2 per hour or less working from less affluent countries. Even if you stay within the US, it's still less expensive to get a VA from the middle of Kansas than it is to hire someone local in Manhattan.

There can be a higher level of talent. You can find a first-class MBA in India for less cost than a high-school graduate in many areas in the US.

A time-zone difference can benefit your work flow. You might find it desirable to have your VA working while you sleep. Then you can base your work on what the VA has completed or discovered. However, if you need to speak directly to your VA regularly, a time-zone difference might be a hassle.

There's great flexibility with VA's. You could have three VA's working for you this week and then only have one next week as your workload changes.

The primary disadvantage of a VA is the inability to perform physical tasks. Sometimes it's incredibly convenient to have someone run out and mail a package, take the company car into the shop, or run some other errands.

ASSESS YOUR NEEDS

It's difficult to find a good assistant if you're unsure of what you need. Consider the repetitive tasks that are necessary to market your business effectively.

Do you just want someone to make cold calls and set up appointments? Or do you require someone that can cold call and possibly close a sale?

Perhaps you're in need of someone to post classified ads and return phone calls. Maybe you are looking for a person to build web sites and do internet marketing. Your ideal VA might require familiarity with social media tools, such as Facebook and Twitter.

The list of possible tasks that a virtual assistant can perform for you is nearly endless. What's important is to understand how you can fit a VA into your business plan. Then you can look for a person who fits with your goals and can assist you with completing various tasks.

FINDING A VIRTUAL ASSISTANT

There are many options for finding and assessing a virtual assistant. **It's a little more challenging to assess someone without seeing them in-person, but it's not difficult to find a top-notch candidate.**

Explore the following approaches when searching for a virtual assistant:

The do-it-yourself approach is likely to be the most cost effective. Although it might be cheaper to find your own virtual assistant, it's also likely to take more time.

When you search for a virtual assistant on your own, you're likely to find plenty of qualified candidates.

You can post ads and search through the offerings at sites like Odesk, Elance, Freelancer, and Guru.

Post classified ads on Craigslist. Nearly everyone uses Craigslist now and many qualified professionals are looking for extra work to keep themselves busy.

Ask around. You might find that you have friends or family that could provide the assistance you need. They might also know the perfect person for your requirements.

Use a virtual staffing agency. There are many services that can match you up with a great virtual assistant.

One example of this type of service is HYPERLINK "http://www.virtualstafffinder.com" www.virtualstafffinder.com.

Consider using a dedicated virtual assistant service.
These are companies that actually employ virtual assistants
and will charge you for using one of their VA's.

**Hire several at first. The best way to find a great VA is
to hire a few of them and give each of them a few tasks
that will allow you to assess their skills.**

You might even give all of them the exact same task and be
able to compare apples-to-apples.

After this brief trial period, you can simply hire the best
one for the long term.

HOW TO MANAGE YOUR VIRTUAL ASSISTANT

This is when your real work begins. Managing other
individuals is never easy, but trying to do it remotely can be
even more challenging.

**These tips will help to ensure that you and your VA
are on the same page:**

Set up tools that make communication easy and effective. Some of these might be common sense, but others are less obvious.

Create an email message system that decreases the opportunity for miscommunication. All communications should also include the specific job at hand.

Have a way of communicating in real time. There are numerous chat clients and web camera communication systems available. Get at least two set up so you'll have a backup if one goes down.

Initially, assign clearly defined tasks that require minimum judgment from the VA. It's easier to get your feet wet with a new VA if you assign tasks that can be accomplished through the communication systems you've set up.

After you have a better feel for your virtual assistant's skills, you can unleash them on the world.

Have clear expectations about your requirements and deadlines. If certain items have a higher priority, make that clear to your virtual assistant. **Set specific deadlines and stick to them.**

Be realistic. You might think that a task takes you 40 minutes, but it actually takes 75 minutes. Time yourself doing the task you're planning to assign and then be reasonable.

You're bound to be faster doing something that you've already done 300 times than someone will be when they're doing it for the first time.

Be aware of language differences. Assuming that you're looking for a VA to work in a business that uses the English language, be aware that your VA's first language might not be English. Also be aware that American English can be different from Indian and British English. Even our neighbors to the north use different spellings for many words.

A virtual assistant can take on those repetitive busy tasks that prevent you from spending your time on the critical tasks that really define your business. **Marketing tasks fit the bill perfectly for a VA because it's one of those things that must be done consistently to really reap the benefits.**

Find a VA that has the skill-set you are seeking. Then, develop a list of tasks to be performed. If you've chosen a competent virtual assistant, you'll find yourself spending less time on the busy work and more time on the tasks that matter. Even better, your profits should increase.

CHAPTER 5

PERSONAL SHOPPING

A common goal for most of us is to bring in as much income as possible each month. Finding alternative activities we enjoy that can also create an additional income is about as good as it gets when it comes to earning extra money.

Have you ever considered starting a second income as a personal shopper?

WHAT IS PERSONAL SHOPPING?

Personal shopping is where you're paid to help others locate and obtain items they want to purchase. Because of the fast pace of our lives today, many are looking for ways to cut corners and reduce the amount of tasks they do themselves.

Frankly, those who are wealthy often prefer to pay someone else to do the "mundane" tasks they would rather not do, which oftentimes involves shopping for themselves or buying gifts for others.

For example, perhaps an elderly lady, Ms. Adams, no longer enjoys doing her holiday shopping and would instead prefer to deal with a personal shopper who selects gifts for her loved ones.

As a personal shopper, you'll arrange a meeting with Ms. Adams. Compile a list of the people Ms. Adams wants you to shop for, helpful information about each person, and any gift suggestions. Then, you'll shop for and purchase the items for her.

Sometimes, the client will accompany you and you'll work together to select items. It is the responsibility of the personal shopper to provide feedback on items the client selects.

If Ms. Adams does not accompany you, then you'll return to her home with the requested items. Ms. Adams will approve the items and then pay you for the items, as well as for your services.

Another type of personal shopper is hired to run personal errands for clients, such as picking up medication, paying the electric bill, and other such tasks.

HOW YOU GET PAID

You have various options when it comes to deciding how you'll charge your clients. Many personal shoppers charge a percentage of the overall bill for the items they purchase on behalf of the client.

For example, if you spent $400 on the gifts Ms. Adams requested, you could charge her an additional 20% of the total, plus a one-time fee of $10. You'd earn $90 from this job.

In the event you completed a list of errands for a client, you might want to consider charging a flat hourly rate for those types of services.

PERKS

An especially nice feature of being a personal shopper is its flexibility: you can do it as a temporary job or even a second job, by scheduling meetings and shopping trips outside of your full-time work schedule.

Plus, you decide what type of shopping you're willing to do for others. For example, clothing and accessories might be your forte while furniture is not.

TRICKS OF THE TRADE: TIPS FOR SUCCESS

As with any business, it's recommended you familiarize yourself with the necessary tools used by a personal shopper. This will allow you to complete personal shopping tasks as efficiently as possible and to start building up your bank account quickly.

The following tools are essential for a personal shopper:

A dependable vehicle, a car with a large trunk for storage is required. One that gets excellent gas mileage is a plus! A small van would also work.

A Global Positioning System (GPS) for your vehicle. You'll be required to arrive on time and do some local traveling as a personal shopper. Having directions you can quickly access makes a GPS a must-have.

A cell phone, situations will arise when you'll want to call your client to clarify their wishes or inquire about certain items you plan to purchase for them. A cell phone is an invaluable tool for easily and instantly contacting your client.

To go even further, if you inform your clients of the day and approximate time (morning or afternoon) you'll be doing their shopping, you can ask them to be reachable by cell phone during those hours.

Business cards and pamphlets to advertise your business. Business cards and pamphlets are extremely important for any business owner.

The pamphlet, which could be a simple one-page hand-out, should include your name and all of your contact information, including phone numbers, an email address, and even an office address, if you like. It should also contain a short blurb about what you can do for prospective clients.

Include your pricing information and some examples of the services you offer to clients. It may be a good idea to establish policies on how you'll handle item returns. For example, what will you charge for returning an item to the retailer?

Business cards are small, compact, and still a very important way to advertise any business. The same contact information from your pamphlet should be on your business cards. Potential clients will often ask for one of your cards.

A simple marketing plan, how will you get the word out about your personal shopping business? Check with local radio stations, as they often interview local business owners.

Look for venues frequented by potential clients, such as local coffee shops and grocery stores, and drop off a stack of business cards at those establishments.

Consider canvasing your neighborhood on foot to introduce yourself door-to-door. Give out your pamphlets and business cards to your neighbors and friends.

Client Information Forms. A client information form contains all the tidbits of information you require to appropriately complete personal shopping duties for a client.

It includes the client's contact information and statement about what they want you to do as their personal shopper. The form should also include the names of who you're shopping for, as well as their relationship to your client, their age, and their interests.

You should also have a space to write out the client's suggested gifts to purchase for each person on the list.

Keep in mind you'll often be shopping for the client as well.

Establish friendly relationships with local retailers. Regardless of where you live, educate yourself about the retailers in your area. Know who carries the widest variety and largest inventory of the items you are likely to purchase.

Establish connections with retail sales managers in departments you plan to shop in frequently. Know names of sales assistants and ensure they know your name.

Keep a file drawer for receipts. If you place copies of receipts and information into a file labeled with the name of each client, you'll know just where to find it in the future.

It is also imperative to have a file labeled "Tax Deductions" where you can store all your gas and oil receipts, cell phone bills, and any other receipts related to your business.

QUALITIES AND CHARACTERISTICS OF A SUCCESSFUL PERSONAL SHOPPER

If you have, or can develop, certain characteristics, you will make a great personal shopper.

If you are able to answer "yes" to the following questions, a career as a personal shopper might be just perfect for you:

Do you consider yourself a "people person?"

Are you able to make new acquaintances easily?

Do you possess a helpful nature and the ability to reach out to others?

Do you have excellent listening skills?

Do you have at least some retail experience?

Are you always on time and aware of how important promptness is?

Do you possess a knack for selecting items others will like?

Are you up on all the newest styles, fashions, electronics, gadgetry, and furnishings?

Do you love to shop and investigate new trends?

MOVING FORWARD

Regardless of the type of work you do full-time, you just might have what it takes to develop a second career as a personal shopper.

If shopping is one of your favorite activities and you have the necessary tools to carry out the job, perhaps you should consider becoming a personal shopper.

If you have the qualities necessary to be successful at this type of work, then you could quite possibly have a highly profitable adventure waiting for you just around the corner!

CHAPTER 6

SETTING UP A PART-TIME OFFICE CLEANING BUSINESS

How would you like to start a part-time business that doesn't require much money to get started or have many overhead costs? A part-time office cleaning business can be a great way to get started as an entrepreneur and also has the added benefit of being tremendously scalable.

With this type of business, you can ultimately grow extremely large and make a lucrative income.

Follow these steps to get your office cleaning business up and running:

Decide what type of businesses to target. There are many issues to consider. Would you like to clean large office buildings or small? Would you prefer to service small businesses? Schools?

If you're taking on this business alone, with no other employees, you're likely going to have to start small. This can be a good thing. It will provide you with time to learn the business and become successful. You'll learn how to deal with clients, what supplies you'll need, and how to manage your finances.

As you get more experienced and earn the funds to hire additional employees, you can target larger buildings.

Also consider the hours you're available. Assuming you already have a full-time job, you'll need to work around your other work schedule.

Keep in mind that most businesses won't want you there during their normal business hours, so you'll probably have to clean at night.

Think about how much work you can handle. Start small until you have a good idea of how much extra workload you can add to your routines.

Name your business. Since your clients are professionals, you'll probably want to name your business something that sounds professional. If you want to keep your business local, you might incorporate your city name into your business name. Avoid trying to be cute. You want the give the project a professional image.

Get your business license and a bank account. Different

states have different rules and laws about business licenses. You may only have to get a DBA (doing business as) name, which is usually very inexpensive. However, getting your business registered as a limited liability corporation will limit your liability should something happen.

If you can afford an attorney, it might be a wise investment at this point. What would happen if you or your employee knocked a client's computer off a desk?

It would be best to get a separate business account at your bank. Mixing personal and business funds can be an issue, especially at tax time. What if something happens and your single account gets frozen due to business issues? You wouldn't be able to access your personal funds either.

Shop around for the best deals. Some bank accounts have higher minimum balance requirements and higher fees.

Find liability insurance. Most commercial clients will require you to have insurance. Most businesses will ask to see your insurance certificate and may even have a minimum amount of coverage they require. $500,000 worth of coverage will be enough in most instances.

Your local insurance agent should be able to provide you with the advice and coverage you require. Liability coverage is not expensive.

If you have employees, a bond is a good idea. A bond primarily protects you if an employee steals from your client. Bonds are inexpensive and offer good protection from unscrupulous employees.

Set your rates. Determining what you're going to charge your clients for cleaning services is the last step to complete before you actually begin operating your business. There are a couple things to consider:

What is the competition charging? With a few phone calls and a little research, you can determine a good average rate for your area. It might be smart to set your rates a little lower until you build up a sufficient client base.

What hourly rate do you want to earn? When you have an interested potential client, consider how many hours a job is likely to take and set your fee accordingly. Remember to consider the cost of travel and supplies!

Advertise. Advertising and marketing are always important, especially when first starting a business. You can't be hired if nobody even knows that your business exists. Consider some of the following options:

Phone calls/mail/flyers/brochures. These are all direct

contact methods. Flyers are inexpensive to create and can be inexpensive to distribute if you do it yourself. Consider faxing your information to potential clients. Brochures are also inexpensive in significant quantities. The cheapest option is to just pick up the phone.

Website. Every business should have a website. With WordPress, anyone can put up a good looking website in short order. Visit wordpress.org for details.

Newspapers and magazines, print media formats can be good advertising tools, but they can also be expensive. The effectiveness can depend a lot on the local area.

Online advertising. Advertising online can be inexpensive or even free. There are a variety of places to advertise online. It would be great to link your advertisement back to your webpage.

Business cards, car magnets, or other forms, do everything you can to get your business out in front of people by giving them your contact information.

Give estimates. Anyone who contacts you should be offered a free estimate. Always be on time and dress professionally.

Use a tape measure to determine room size. You'll quickly learn how long it takes to vacuum, sweep, or mop a particular size room.

Find out exactly what your client wants cleaned. If possible, find out what they liked or disliked about the previous cleaning service. Use this information wisely.

Complete your bid within a few days. You should include a cover letter, your bid sheet, copy of your insurance, and several business cards. They might pass your card on to another business owner.

Start cleaning! Ensure you get high quality cleaning supplies, but also watch the cost. There is bound to be at least one janitorial supply company in your local area. Also consider green cleaning products, as they don't emit harmful fumes. Do a great job, but manage your time well.

After the initial cleaning, ask your client to review the work and offer feedback. It's much easier (in most cases) to keep a client than it is to find a new one. Strive to make each client happy.

If you have employees, review the quality of their work on a regular basis and make your expectations and those of the business owner you are cleaning for very clear.

Grow your business, cautiously. Expanding your business can be exciting, but be careful. Sometimes costs can quickly get out of control. Managing multiple clients and employees can be time consuming as well. Continue to add clients and employees at a rate you can handle.

Know when to cut a client loose. Not all clients are good clients. For every 10 clients, 2 will probably be more trouble than they're worth. It's not worth spending all your time managing those two clients and their issues. Simply let them go and find two better clients. Don't be afraid to cull your duds. The same goes for your employees.

Setting up your own part-time cleaning business is something anyone can do. It requires a minimum amount of money and knowledge to get started. The best advice is to start small and then scale-up as you gain the expertise to grow efficiently and intelligently.

A cleaning business can provide a great supplemental income and it also has the potential to grow into a full-time business where it could become your sole income.

CHAPTER 7

LET YOUR HOUSE PAY FOR ITSELF

One of the best strategies to boost your incoming dollars is to creatively think of ways to reduce your home mortgage or monthly rental payment. **Your monthly mortgage or rental amount is likely the largest recurring expense you have.**

So, utilizing your home to make some extra dollars is a wise thing to do. Consider these suggestions to accumulate money from your home:

Take in a roommate or renter. If you have a larger house or condo that has at least one extra bedroom, you could rent out one of the bedrooms to a student or single working person.

Even if you charged them $75-$100 a week for the bedroom, including a shelf in the refrigerator and kitchen privileges, you'd end up with roughly $300-$400 extra a month. You can apply those dollars toward your house payment.

You'd shave costs off of your monthly mortgage. Plus, you'd be helping the other person.

Rent out your home occasionally. Another way to earn with your home is to rent out your house to others for short stints, like vacations, holidays, and special events. It's possible for you to get enough cash on a regular basis to pay your mortgage at least some of the time whenever you rent out your home a few times a year.

If you live in a tourist town, renting your home out during the high tourist season for three or four weeks a year could provide you with a nice tidy bundle to apply toward your home loan.

Perhaps you live in a community that has a large sporting complex that holds many state or national events or where people come to see the natural landscapes and fall colors.

You could stay with friends and family for just a few short weeks a year while renting out your home for as much as $1,500-$2,000 a week to those who wish to see the sporting events or enjoy the colorful foliage in the fall.

If you prefer, when you go on vacation, rent out your home to someone who wants to vacation in your town and then use the cash to cover your vacation costs. Websites like Vacation Rentals by Owners (VRBO) make it easy for you to list your home for the exact period of time you wish to make it available for rental.

Renovate your home to include a small apartment unit. If you live in a two-story home or a home with a basement, you may have a virtual gold mine. Do some renovations to include a small living area, kitchenette, bathroom, and bedroom.

If you have a large upstairs area, it may be easier than you think to hook two or three of the rooms together and have a kitchen installed. Voila! You now have a small apartment that you could rent out for several hundred dollars a month.

The same goes for a finished basement. You could make a studio apartment with open living, dining, and kitchen area with a bedroom area installed behind one wall.

Even though both of these plans would involve you doing a lot of the work (tearing out walls, painting, and the like) and then paying upfront for the renovations you're unable to do yourself (wiring, plumbing, and cabinet installation), you stand to make hundreds monthly once you rent out the space.

Purchase a multi-unit property. Another way to let your

home pay for itself is to buy a multi-unit property like a duplex or triplex. You could live in in one unit and rent out the other(s). Then, use the rent from the other units' tenants to pay your entire mortgage payment on the property each month.

Owning and living in a multi-unit property allows you to live "rent-free" while you build up equity in the property.

You'll also learn how to become a landlord while banking some extra bucks.

In fact, you may even have extra money left over from the tenants' rent payments after paying your monthly mortgage payments. Then, you can use that income to invest in more real estate, which then pays for itself with its own renters, too.

Or you might want to use the extra income to start "flipping homes"—buying bank-owned or short sale properties to fix up and sell.

However you decide to use it, the multi-unit property purchase plan is great for getting you the cash for investing in your first real estate deal, regardless of what you do with it after you buy it. Plus, you'll have the opportunity to "stick your toe" into the waters of becoming a landlord and managing a real estate investment.

Ultimately, your home will be paying for itself when you buy and live in a multi-unit property.

It's exciting to think about how your home could be the key to your future financial freedom. Take some time to explore all the ways you might be able to let your home pay for itself. When the money starts coming in, you'll be glad you did.

SPECIAL FACTORS TO CONSIDER WHEN YOU PLAN

TO BOOST YOUR INCOME WITH YOUR HOME

As you're mulling over the above strategies to let your house pay for itself, keep in mind these tidbits of information:

Extra money each month. With some of the above suggestions, even though you may not make enough to pay every monthly mortgage payment, you'll surely bring in the extra money to pay a portion of your mortgage payments or pay down your principal to pay off the mortgage more quickly.

Invest in an attorney. Another factor to consider is meeting with a real estate attorney to help you draw up a contractual agreement form to use with renters to ensure you understand one another. Spelling out the specific aspects of your arrangements in advance can help prevent troublesome situations later.

Keep an open mind. When it comes to earning money from your house, it's a good idea to ponder doing things that you wouldn't have considered in the past. For example, you may have trouble imagining taking in a stranger to rent one of your bedrooms.

However, you could use word of mouth with friends and neighbors to find a trusted college student or young professional who's just starting out. If you do end up trying it out (renting out a room), you may be pleasantly surprised to see how simple it is to adjust to sharing your home with another person.

The added income could really take the pressure off paying a high mortgage payment.

Allow yourself to try some new ways to boost your income. Who knows where you could go financially after you develop an additional stream of steady income?

A cautionary note. It's important to carry the necessary liability insurance and include the extra income in your taxes if you decide to undertake some of these suggestions. Check with your city's coding and zoning officials or an attorney with your questions.

It may be hard to imagine that your home could actually be paying for itself. But as you can see, it is possible. With some work on your part, you can make hundreds of extra dollars monthly. Using your home to gain more income can get you out of a financial jam. Join the thousands of people who enjoy extra income from their homes. Your financially abundant future is waiting.

CHAPTER 8

HOW TO START YOUR OWN PART-TIME LANDSCAPING BUSINESS

Landscaping can be the perfect part-time business. **Lawn care can even be a year-round source of income, if you live in the certain climates.** Those that live in cooler climates might consider adding a snow removal service in the winter months. The late fall period can be a good time to offer leaf removal services.

While landscaping isn't a complicated endeavor, having a plan before getting started can make your life and business venture much easier.

Research

Before starting your landscaping business, it's important to do some research. **When you do the appropriate research before starting your business, the odds for success are greater and the number of surprises can be greatly reduced.**

Consider these items when researching the viability of your landscaping business:

What services are being offered by your competitors? Take a look at what's being offered in your area. Can you offer something different than competing companies? Are there required services that would be difficult for you to offer?

How much is your competition charging? If you can't readily find out how much your competition is charging, call some of your competitors and ask for some quotes for various services.

How do other companies present themselves? Are they professional in appearance with new trucks and logos on all their vehicles? Or is the competition primarily a single person with a rusted pick-up truck from the 1970's?

How are other companies marketing? Consider how other companies are making themselves known to potential clients. What is your plan?

How can you be better? After gathering all of that information, find ways that you can make enhancements. Could you be more professional in appearance? Could you offer more reliable service? What about better rates or additional services?

Research is an important part of starting any business. If you're exactly like the other companies, it will be difficult to be successful.

Planning Stage

Now that you know your marketplace, it's time to make a plan. Your plan doesn't have to be perfect, and odds are that it won't be. But you have to start somewhere. **Strive to make your operation better over time as you gain more experience.**

Consider these factors when deciding how to profitably meet the needs of the marketplace:

Figure out how much money you are able to invest. Landscaping doesn't require a great outlay of funds to get started, but it's important to assess your financial situation. **Do your best to avoid taking on any unnecessary debt.**

Get the proper equipment. A vehicle, lawnmower, trimmer, fertilizer spreader, shovel, rake, and wheelbarrow will take care of most of your needs. If you're short on funds, a lawnmower and trimmer are enough to get started.

Find a mower that has the option to bag the clippings. Most modern mulching mowers do a great job without the need for a bag, but some customers will want the clippings to be taken away.

Be sure the trimmer is gas-powered rather than electric. Some customers would prefer to not supply the electricity. Electric trimmers are also limited by the length of your extension cord. They also have less power and are slower. And time is money!

Many great, used items can be found for sale in the various classified ads found online, like at craigslist.org, and in your local publications. It's not unusual to find free items, too.

Think about how you want to organize your business. If you're just mowing a few lawns, you might consider not formalizing your business at all. A sole-proprietorship can be a viable option for small operations, especially if you have limited assets.

A limited-liability corporation will be the best option for most. Your personal assets are protected from any legal actions resulting from your business operations. This will cost a few hundred dollars to get started, however.

Consult a local attorney for advice in how to structure your business.

Consider how you want to be paid. Getting paid is the most important part. It's relatively easy these days to accept debit and credit cards with a smart phone. There are many good options. **The easier you can make it for customers to pay you, the more likely you are to get paid.**

If possible, avoid any co-mingling of business and personal funds. Again, if you're just mowing a few lawns, putting your earnings into your personal bank account is unlikely to be an issue.

However, realize that it's possible to have the bank account you use for business purposes to be frozen in the event of any legal issues. For that reason, separate bank accounts are probably a good idea.

Companies like PayPal make it easy to set up recurring payments. This can be great because you minimize the amount of time you spend collecting your fees. However, be aware that these online companies typically charge high-fees for their services.

Remember to provide an invoice for your clients. Invoice forms can be found in your local office supply stores.

There are many free forms available online, as well.

Figure out how to advertise. Advertising is a critical part of any business. Some forms of advertising are expensive, but many are free or at least very affordable. It's perfectly acceptable to start with the lower-cost forms before moving up to the more expensive options.

It can be surprisingly difficult to rank in the search engines for local search terms. A little research into search engine optimization can really pay off.

Print up some flyers and go door-to-door. Copies are inexpensive, so all it really takes is your time and energy.

Phone book advertising is getting less effective every year, but it can still work with the older generation. Be aware that Yellow Pages advertising is expensive.

There are many free, online advertising opportunities. Craigslist is one of the most well-known.

Post flyers on telephone poles and in other public areas such as grocery store bulletin boards. However, be careful of local ordinances.

Start making money! Answer inquiries from potential customers, schedule the work, and start earning some money.

Respond to potential customers as quickly as possible. Few things shout 'unprofessional' more than not answering your phone and not responding to calls and emails in a timely fashion.

Be professional. Make an effort to sound and appear professional. Landscaping has a relatively low barrier to entry. It's important to do what you can to rise above the competition.

Be on time. If you say you'll mow a lawn or plant a tree at 2:00 pm on Thursday, make every effort to abide by that schedule.

Ensure you get paid. Many service providers struggle to get paid, even your local dentist. Those that sell goods get paid at the time of the sale. Service providers typically get paid after the service has already been provided.

After customers already have the service they want, they lack the motivation to pay. Be diligent with your collection efforts.

Ask for referrals. This is the cheapest advertising around. It doesn't require time or money. **There's no better endorsement than word of mouth.**

Regularly assess your operation and seek ways to make your business even better.

Starting and running a part-time landscaping business is a viable idea. Avoid diving in headfirst without first performing the necessary research. Stand out: try to do things better than your competition and offer services that they don't.

Landscaping can be a lucrative part-time business that can be expanded to full-time once a suitable customer base is in place. If you enjoy the outdoors, consider spending more time outside, making money in your landscaping business.

CHAPTER 9

INCREASE YOUR INCOME WITH CRAIG'S LIST

Craig's List (HYPERLINK "http://www.craigslist.org" www.craigslist.org), is the online equivalent of the newspaper classifieds. Nearly every type of item and service under the sun is available there.

The best part is that the site is free to view and post ads. Of course, there are a few premium advertising options that require a small fee, but it is not required.

The site is hugely popular, so there are opportunities to really make some money with a little bit of work. You may have heard of the high school student that traded his way from a used cell phone to a Porsche. This was all done on Craig's List, and he never spent a dime, he only traded items.

Here are several ways that you can make money with this great site:

Sell your stuff. This is the most obvious way. Take all that stuff in the closets, garage, attic, and basement and get it out of your life and out of your way. Someone out there wants it and would be willing to pay you for it.

If you have real junk that you want to get rid of, things like broken bikes, tree limbs, scrap metal, or similar items, you can usually find someone interested in hauling it away for free. Someone out there fixes bikes or wants wood or scrap metal. You're not making money, but you're saving money by not paying someone to haul it away.

Sell other people's stuff. There are people that make a full-time living from buying stuff at flea markets and yard sales and then selling those items on Craig's List. You need to know the going price for whatever item it is that you're buying. If you have a smart phone, it's easy to check prices.

When you find something that seems like a great deal, pull up the website on your phone and see what similar items are selling for. Be smart about your decisions. Check multiple ads.

If you're already visiting these sales anyway shopping for yourself, why not keep your eyes open for things that you can sell to make money? You can have a good time and make money simultaneously!

Buy and sell stuff from Craig's List. Many people scour the website for great deals, snatch them up, and then improve the item (clean, paint, or repair) or improve the quality of the ad and sell them back on Craig's List.

Sometimes it's simply a matter of patience. You might find a seller that is in a hurry to sell. Those sellers will usually take a lower price than a seller that has the option of waiting. Find those sellers.

This is no different than stock arbitrage. It's like you're in high finance. Imagine bragging to your friends!

Pick up free items on Craig's List and sell them. A common practice is to grab items from the Free section and then sell them. It helps to have a truck, because a lot of these are larger items, like furniture.

Again, improve the item quickly. This most likely means some paint or cleaning. Sell it and find some more stuff.

It pays to move quickly on the free items. Frequently, the owner of the item will simply leave it out by the curb and it's 'first-come first-serve'. Stay on top of the ads and be prepared to move quickly.

Sell your services. If there is something you can do well for someone else, and you have the time to do it, put your own ad on there. Can you build websites? Clean homes? Walk dogs? Do taxes?

Secrets of Making a Great Craig's List Ad

Follow these tips for writing an effective ad:

Use a great headline. Address your customer's problem. You don't have a lot of room to work with, but give the title some time and effort. Look at the other ads and notice those that stand out to you.

Use pictures. Ads with pictures are much more successful than those without images. People want to see what they're buying. If you're selling a service, some simple clip art related to the service makes your ad look more professional.

Consider using HTML. Even if you're not a programmer, there are lots of free programs on the Internet that will allow you to create a visually pleasing advertisement. Then you can simply cut and paste the code into Craig's List. Anyone can do it.

Spend some time on the text of the ad. To get some ideas, look at what some other people have done. Write like you know what you're talking about and be clear. You'll find that some people have one, long endless paragraph that's difficult to read – these serve as examples of what not to do.

Give them the critical information that you would want to know. For example, if you were to read an ad about a couch, you'd want to know the condition, color, style, and shape or size. You'd also want to see a picture of it. Include this same type of information in your ads and make it easy to find.

Consider the best time to post it. Many of the categories get a lot of postings each day. The postings that are near the top get a lot more views than the ones further down the page. The amount of traffic varies throughout the day as well. The smart tactic is to post your ad when there are likely to be a lot of people online and looking.

Early in the day can be good. About 9:00 or so in the morning is a good time. Everyone has made it to work but they're still not quite ready to really get busy. Many people sit at their desk at peruse the ads.

Lunch time or just after lunch also makes a lot of sense. Many people eat lunch at their desk and get on the Internet. Others get online immediately after going out to lunch. This is another great time to post.

The evening around 9:00 pm is another good time. The kids are in bed, and many people get online in the evening before going to bed themselves.

You'll need multiple ads. Craig's List currently only allows 3 ads to be posted per account per day. You can only get as many accounts as you have verifiable phone numbers. The other catch is that you can only post the same ad every 48 hours.

To create multiple ads that aren't picked up by their system, you don't need to change a lot from your first advertisement. You'll have to play around with it to see just how much. But you'll need 6 versions if you're going to post it 3 times per day.

After 48 hours are past, you can simply start reposting your previous ads. There is an option to do this on the website.

Answer promptly. The default method of making contact is via email. You can choose to include your phone number, but if you do, it's important to return calls as soon as possible. You don't want them running off to buy someone else's stuff!

Be persistent. Test different ads and keep posting them. It might take a week to sell something. It's just a matter of the right person seeing it. You never know when that will be.

Craig's List provides many opportunities to make money on the side. There is even the possibility of making a full-time income. Take a look at all your options and go for it!

All of the methods require some work, but the money you earn per hour of work can be impressive.

Do you think it would be all that difficult to find a couch for sale for $200 that you could then sell for $400? Or do you think you could pick up a free desk and sell it for $100? That's pretty easy. You would be shocked at how many people are making several hundred dollars or more each month.

With some very part-time work, you could easily pay for a great vacation for the whole family each year.

Happy posting!

CHAPTER 10

HOW TO WHOLESALE REAL ESTATE IN YOUR SPARE TIME

Wholesaling real estate can be a great part-time activity. You can easily make another $25k-$50k per year. It's relatively simple, but you have to work it hard.

In a nutshell, you put houses under contract for less than 70% of their retail value and then sell the contract to investors / renovators at 70%. They then sell or rent the house on the retail market.

You can make money without ever owning the house and without needing money or good credit.

Here are few definitions you'll need to know before we get started:

MLS = Multiple-listing service. This is the database that real estate agents use to list houses. Investigate how you can gain access yourself. There's always a way. At the very least, you'll need a friendly real estate agent person to help you.

There is a ton of information in the MLS that will be invaluable.

ARV = After-repair value. This is the retail value of a home after it has received any needed repairs.

Comps = Comparables. These are the sales prices of nearby houses that are similar in size and quality. You can get these from your local real estate agent. You can also find the information from the local government, depending on your state. In some states, the information is only available on the MLS.

Now let's move on to the good stuff.

Find Your Buyers First

Ideally, you're going to spend your time finding the properties and not spend your time trying to sell them. The best way to accomplish this is to find your buyers first. You will frequently hear that if you have a great deal, it's easy to sell it. That's not always true!

Try these ideas to compile a buyers list before you start making offers:

Find buyers on the MLS that have paid cash. Call your friendly realtor and ask them for a list of houses that have been bought in the last 2 months for cash. From those listings, it's a simple matter to find the buyers.

Check out the county clerk's office or the local tax records. It will depend on your state, but there is a simple way to find these folks if you ask.

Once you've found them, give them a call and say, "Hi, I'm a real estate wholesaler. I was wondering if you're actively buying properties." Then ask what types of properties they're looking for. Get their phone number and email address – you'll need it later.

Run a fake ad. This is a common tactic. Put an ad on HYPERLINK "http://www.craigslist.org" www.craigslist.org that says something like this: 3 bdrm / 2 bath. 50 cents on the dollar. Must sell. Cash only. Nice house.

The types of investors that you're looking will call so fast your head will spin. Let them know that the house already sold but you'll let them know the next time you have something. Get their name, phone, and email.

Call 'houses for rent' ads. The owners of these rental houses are prefect buyers for your properties. Call the ads and ask them if they are looking for houses to buy. Again, find out what they want and get their phone and email address.

Contact title companies. Title companies know everyone. While they might not be willing to give you names, they will certainly pass on your name to the appropriate people.

Join the local real estate club. Every city has at least one. Join and talk to people. Find out who actively buys or rehabs and then get in contact with them.

Now you have 5 ways to find buyers. Keep in mind that you only really need 1 or 2 good buyers, though it never hurts to have more.

When you have a property to sell, shoot-off an email with all the relevant details of the property (bcc everyone). With a good buyers list, you should be able to sell a property in a few days, at most.

Don't be bashful about approaching these people. When you approach the right people, they will be overjoyed that you found them.

Finding the Properties & Sellers

The types of properties you're going to be looking for will depend on your buyers. You just go out and find whatever it is they want. Typically though, the most common properties will be from 50% of the median home price to the median home price in your area.

So if your median home price is $120,000, you'll be looking at properties that would sell (in good shape) for $60k to $100k.

Keep in mind that what you're really looking for are the right owners. These are owners that are either forced to sell or owners that just desperately want to get rid of a property.

These owners could be:

In serious financial difficulty, some people need to sell immediately and really need your help.

Out of state owners. Sometimes people move out of state and leave a home behind. Owning the home becomes too expensive or too much hassle. They may have inherited the house and just want it out of their lives.

Disgruntled landlords. Some landlords just want out and they want out today.

The trick is to find these owners. Here are few ideas:

Hang bandit signs in suitable neighborhoods. These are the type of signs we're talking about: HYPERLINK "http://www.dirtcheapsigns.com/yard_signs" dirtcheapsigns.com/yard_signs. All you need is a sign that says "We Buy Houses" and your phone number. Hang them up on telephone poles or mount them on stakes.

Run ads on HYPERLINK "http://www.craigslist.org" craigslist.org. Run an ad stating that you buy houses for cash and can close quickly. Keep running it over and over.

Call, email, and/or send a postcard to local realtors and attorneys. Again, let them know that you can close quickly for cash. Offer a finder's fee.

Look at bankruptcy and foreclosure filings. Contact these folks and make an offer on their house.

Find owners of abandoned properties. Every time you see an abandoned property, track down the owners and ask them if they'd like to sell. A great person to ask is the local mail carrier for that neighborhood. They see all the houses and know who isn't getting any mail. Offer some money for leads that pan out.

Negotiate

Usually, you don't have to do a lot of negotiating, just to stick to your numbers. Keep in mind that you want to have your first offer rejected. If they say 'yes,' you'll always wonder how low they would've been willing to go! You'll need to find comps to determine the market value of the house.

Repair values can be determined by getting some free estimates from contractors.

Your highest offer should be: $(65\% \times ARV)$ - repairs.

So a house that is worth $120k in great shape, but needs $10k in repairs would have a high offer of $68,000. That's $0.65 \times \$120,000 = \$78,000$ - $10,000 = \$68,000$.

Your starting offer should be no more than: (50% × ARV) - repairs. In our example, that would be $50,000.

You might be asking yourself, "Who in the world is going to sell me their house for half-price?" The answer is: not many people, but there will be some. You just have to keep asking. You won't really understand until you do your first deal.

The right owner will be so happy for your help that they are likely to be crying while they are thanking you. Then you'll understand.

Close & Sell

Once you have an offer accepted, you need to get really busy:

Immediately start selling the house. Take pictures, get the comps together, and send off an email to all your buyers with all the details they need.

Immediately contact a title company to start the title work. If there is a problem with the property, you want to find out ASAP.

Get your money! Ideally, you'll 'assign' the contract to your buyer. This simply means that you assign all your rights in that contract to your buyer. In exchange for that assignment, your buyer gives you money.

Typically, you should get the difference between the contract price and (70% x ARV) - repairs. Investors should be willing to give you 70%. So the better price you negotiate, the more money you're going to make.

To clarify, a house worth $100k ARV that needs no repairs, should earn you $10k if you got it under contract for $60k. $100k x 70% = $70k. 70k-60k=10k. Understand that you're not likely to get paid until closing. Most investors won't give you the money unless everything works out, which is fair.

Repeat!

Keys to Success

Once you have an offer accepted, you need to get really busy:

Realize that it's a numbers game. You will get told 'no' a lot. It's not unheard of for a beginner to have to make 100 offers or more to get one 'yes'.

In time, you'll learn which homes and owners are more likely to result in a signed contract. Don't let all the rejection get you down. Someone will be happy to sell his house to you.

Never stop marketing. Each day, try to do something to market your business. This type of investing is almost entirely a marketing business. Never forget that.

Get the proper forms. There are tons of legal forms available online. You also should be able to get forms from your real estate investing club. Depending on your state, an attorney might be a good idea.

Conclusion

Being a real estate wholesaler is tough, but doable. Investigate the details on your own.

There are a lot of great articles online that can fill in the gaps, but don't get too carried away reading and learning. The part that makes you money is taking action.

Stick to your numbers and you can't go wrong.

Good luck!

CHAPTER 11

HOW TO USE ABANDONED STORAGE UNITS TO AUGMENT YOUR INCOME

Can you make money with storage units like the folks on TV?

Buying and selling stuff has been a respectable way to make a living since the beginning of human kind. Just because it's been around forever, though, doesn't always mean that it's easy. Just like anything else, there are some fundamental rules to follow for the best results.

On the most basic level, you must acquire items that people actually want. You must also get these items at a price that permits you to make a profit when you sell them. If you can just accomplish these two things, you will be successful.

One great place to find such items is at abandoned or foreclosed storage units.

All you really need to get started is a way to haul the items back home and a few hundred dollars.

Acquiring the Merchandise

Fortunately for you, the US is full of packrats that can't let go of their excess stuff. Businesses and people will store this excess stuff and many eventually fall behind on their payments or simply decide that they don't want it anymore.

The owners of the storage facilities essentially take control of the unit and auction the contents off to the highest bidder. These units can range from 25 square feet, with few items, up to several hundred square feet, with a whole treasure trove.

Use these strategies to successfully profit from these auctions:

Find the auctions. Do some Google searches and call all the storage facilities in your area. Ask when the next auction is scheduled. You'll find that the larger places have them regularly, and the smaller ones only hold them as needed. Be sure to call the smaller places back at least once a month.

They might advertise the auctions in a local paper. Find out what paper they use and keep your eyes open.

Some storage facilities actually just sell the contents of the unit to anyone that will bring the rent current. If that's the case, ask to be put on their list of potential buyers. Ask about the process. How do they choose between multiple buyers?

Show up at the auctions. Arrive a little early to figure out what's going on. Ideally, you'll have a pickup or some other type of large truck. Vans can be okay for most items. You can always rent a truck if needed.

A strong partner is nice to have because some of the items might be quite heavy. How is your back? A dolly or hand truck is nice to have, too.

Bring gloves and a flashlight. It might be dark and some items might have exposed nails or screws or just be filthy. A pen, paper, and calculator can be handy, too. You'll also need a lock.

Inspect. Different storage facilities have different rules. Typically, they'll open the door and give everyone a couple of minutes to inspect the unit from outside. You aren't allowed inside. You might be able to see everything, but frequently things will be in boxes. You might get to see inside some of the boxes or you might not.

Keep a tally on a pad of paper what you think the items are worth. You'll have to guess at some things. A smart phone and a quick check on eBay can be a big help.

Set your maximum bid. This should be about 50% of what you think everything in the unit is worth. If you have a lot of doubt about the value of the items, don't bid. There's always another storage unit and another day.

If you smell mildew or anything else that smells bad, it's probably best to pass on that unit. The same goes for obvious signs of water damage.

Bid. It might be a good idea to sit back and watch the bidding on the first couple of storage units. There is an art to bidding at auctions, so go slowly at first. Remember not to bid more than 50% of what it's worth.

The auctions are usually live auctions but occasionally silent auctions are used. The pace is usually slower than most other auctions you've seen. The auctioneer will usually be the storage facility manager or owner.

Winning, sorting, and repairing. When you win an auction, you can usually settle up and take possession of your treasures immediately. You typically have 24 hours to get everything out of there, so don't waste any time. It's time to start sorting.

There is frequently a cleaning deposit that must be paid. It will be returned if the unit is completely cleaned out and swept before the 24 hours are up. Your refunded deposit might be mailed to you in the form of a check.

There's almost always some stuff that's just worthless. Leave all the trash for now. You'll need to take it to the dump eventually, but first, get all the good stuff home. Any clean items in good shape that have no value can be donated to Goodwill or someplace similar.

Start hauling the good stuff back home. An alternative is to rent a storage unit for a month and keep everything there. Just a month! Don't get lazy or you'll be in the same situation as the person who owned the stuff before you.

Try out all of the electronics and other powered items. If it works, great! If it doesn't, try to figure out what it will take to get it working again.

Sell, sell, and sell. Get a good idea of what each item is worth. There are several places to check. These include craigslist.org, the newspaper, yard sales, eBay, and flea markets. Find the most lucrative places to sell your items.

Remember your time, too. It might be better to sell something in the newspaper rather than spending all the time to go to a flea market. Only you know what your time is worth.

Some full-time storage auction folks actually set up a small retail location to sell their items. It's worth considering if you decide to get really serious. Having a retail location entails another set of responsibilities and expenses as well, so consider these carefully in your plan.

Some things will sell better in some places than others. Large common items probably won't sell well on eBay. Something that is easy to ship or uncommon will probably fare better in an online auction.

A lot of little, inexpensive items are probably perfect for a yard sale or a flea market. Read up about flea markets – it's a whole world unto itself.

Storage unit auctions have become quite popular with the new TV shows that focus on this type of activity. You can be part of the excitement and make some extra money.

Every once in a while, you're going to hit it big and find something in a box that's worth $1,000 or more! It might be cash, a coin collection or baseball cards. Sooner or later, you'll hit it big.

Find the auctions and check one out just for fun before you consider bidding. Remember that you'll need a way to transport the items home and might need some strong help. Bring a flashlight, hand truck, gloves, a pen, and paper. Figure out what the storage unit is likely to be worth and only bid up to 50% of that amount.

All that's left is to sell your items. Find the best place to sell your stuff and avoid taking too much time. Spending hours to make another $10 just isn't worth it.

You can do this! Get started today and follow these guidelines to gain some experience and garner your first successes. As you learn what works best for you, you'll enjoy the extra income.

CHAPTER 12

HOW TO MAKE MONEY
WITH YOUR PASSION

You might have heard of others enjoying a fun and fulfilling career related to their passion. They get to spend their time at work doing things they like! What about you? Do you feel as if you're chained to a job you loathe? Do you dream of making money with your passion?

Take heart! Whether you're looking for a fulfilling career or wanting to bring in a second income stream, you can start making plans today for a successful venture making money from your passion.

You can be pretty sure that there is something you love to do that someone would gladly pay you for right now!

There are 3 critical steps to making money with your passion:

Determine all the ways you can monetize your passion.

When you start brainstorming, it's important to do so in a way that moves you toward success.

Most people immediately try to figure out why something won't work. However, if an idea is immediately attacked in this way, the idea tends to be dismissed too quickly.

Every idea – even the best idea – will have challenges associated with it, so record all your ideas without pre-judging them.

Capture as many ideas as you can and then take a few days, maybe even a week, before you approach those ideas critically. Give your brain some time to really ponder on them for a while. A few nights of sleep can create some spectacular results.

Give each idea at least a few minutes of consideration before making a decision. Many excellent ideas are quickly ignored before they are fully investigated.

Be open-minded. Because we associate our passion with 'fun', we don't really consider the financial value that activity might have to others.

Know that you're already an expert. One common challenge you may have is the belief that you don't know enough. But you don't have to be the world's leading expert to be valuable and get paid.

Ask yourself the following question: "Do I know enough about this subject to be able to teach the average person enough to at least get them started?"

If you can answer 'yes', then you know enough to charge people money for your expertise. It's similar to being a math tutor. You might not have a PhD in mathematics, but you could still probably tutor a 5th grader and get paid for it.

There are plenty of people out there that are the equivalent of a 5th grader when it comes to your area of expertise. Being an expert is relative. You are already an expert compared to many.

So, if you could sit down and teach the average person something of value, you already know enough to make money at it. That doesn't mean you shouldn't continue to educate yourself and improve your knowledge and skills. But it does mean that you can get started making money as soon as possible.

Believe you can do the impossible. Many things are commonplace today that were considered to be impossible not that long ago.

The four-minute mile is a common example. It was considered to be impossible for a long time. Then it was accomplished and over 15 additional people did the same thing over the next 3 years. Even high school kids have broken the 4-minute mile barrier.

Of course, making money from your passion is not impossible, but most of us believe that it is. So you have to believe you can do what you feel is impossible.

The easiest way to do this is to surround yourself with people that have already done it. If you can see others that are doing what you want to do, it's like brainwashing in reverse. If you see their reality every day, you'll believe that you can do it, too.

If you can understand how these 3 steps can work for you, it's only a matter of time before you can make your living with your passion!

WHO COULD YOU BE HELPING RIGHT NOW?

Keep in mind that there are things that you love to do that you can do better than the average person. There are also people out there looking for your expertise. If you can simply find each other, you're all set.

Do some research on others who make money with their passion, you'll find that few of them are in any danger of being the next Bill Gates, yet, they do very well! That should be reassuring to you. There are plenty of opportunities for 'regular' people with a passion in a field to excel.

Your biggest obstacle is not a lack of skill, experience, or credentials. It is simply the result of too little creativity or courage. With enough creativity and courage, anything is possible. Focus your energy on those two items. It improves all aspects of your life.

TIPS FOR SUCCESS

Even though you'll be enjoying pursuing your passion in your new business, it's still a business and you'll want to see it bring in profits.

Endeavor to develop these attributes for success in putting your passion to work for you:

Successful people have a relatively accurate perspective about what is possible. Consider this: if your perspective on everything in the world was actually accurate, you'd most likely be wealthier, happier, and more capable of bringing your dreams to life. We all have perceptions that are inaccurate. Strive to imagine what you can really do.

Understand what steps need to be taken. Many of us waste our time on activities that don't have much impact. Determine which activities are priorities for profits and spend more of your time on those activities.

Complete the tasks that you know must be done. Not all business tasks are pleasurable, even if you're passionate about the business. However, successful folks do these necessary tasks quickly and enthusiastically.

MAKE THAT FIRST DOLLAR

Psychologically, it's very powerful to actually make some money at your passion – any money at all! Even if it is just $1, it demonstrates that you're capable of getting paid for your passion. Don't underestimate the power of getting paid for the first time! Be persistent until that first payday happens.

CONCLUSION

Making a great living at your passion is something that anyone can do – even you.

First you must believe that it's possible. Go find some people that are already doing what you want to do. They're out there and finding them with the Internet is easy. By spending time with them, even electronically, you'll begin to believe that you can do the same.

Brainstorm all the possibilities with an open mind. Take a week before you start really looking at the ideas critically. What seems like a bad idea on day 1 can look pretty good on day 8.

Take action and make that first dollar. A simple sale can make all the difference in the world. One dollar and you're off to the races.

Give yourself the chance to make money doing what you really love. You can do it!

CHAPTER 13

HOW TO MAKE $500 FAST IN OFFLINE MARKETING

Offline marketing is all the buzz now and it's not surprising. There are a lot of small businesses that don't really know how to market their businesses effectively online.

Your local dry cleaner or cosmetic dentist probably knows less about online marketing than you think. Even if you're not a computer whiz, it's likely you know enough to provide a valuable service.

While it can be a competitive field, it's not that difficult to make some real money quickly.

Here are several ideas that can help you make money as fast as today:

Target smaller businesses. Businesses with 10 or fewer employees are able to make decisions quickly. Larger businesses are more likely to want to hire someone with demonstrated experience and expertise or need to have meetings to reach a conclusion to use your services

Target businesses that are already advertising in some way. You don't want to have to convince someone about the importance of advertising. You want someone that's already advertising in some fashion. A few good places to find such businesses are:

The Yellow Pages. Yellow Pages ads are quite expensive. Any business with an actual ad as opposed to just the standard listing is a good candidate.

Groupon. Go to their website and search around. Any company with a Groupon deal is already willing to spend money to advertise.

Val-Pak. These usually come in the mail, but there is also a website you can you use to find prospects. The minimum charge to a company for advertising with Val-Pak is around $1,000. These companies see the value of advertising and are willing to spend money on marketing.

Offer a specific service at first. Become known as the gal that makes YouTube videos or the guy that creates mobile websites. Find something that interests you or that you're already good at. Consider these services for inspiration:

Make videos of the business and distribute them to online

video sharing services.

Create websites or mobile versions of their websites.

Set up a blog for the company. Offer to make weekly posts.

Write press releases and submit them to online press release services.

Manage search engine pay-per-click advertising campaigns.

Design Facebook pages.

Handle their social site marketing on Facebook, Twitter, Instagram, or similar sites.

Build their list of customers and prospects and send coupons, ads, or newsletters by using an autoresponder service like Aweber.

Once you've been hired for one service, you can always come back and sell them additional services later.

Contact the businesses offline. Many offline marketers want to find customers online, since a lot of computer people can be a little shy socially. It's much quicker to approach them directly. These ideas make it easier:

Phone. The phone gets much easier with practice. Have a script and just make those calls. There are plenty of scripts available online. A neat trick is to call when you know the business will be closed and simply leave a message! When someone calls you back, you know they're pretty serious.

Flyers or pamphlets. Print up some simple flyers or pamphlets. Pass them out to business owners, saying something like, "I've started a new business and I'm just getting out in the neighborhood to get the word out." Give them your flyer.

Direct mail. There are a lot of services, including the U.S. Postal Service, which will print and mail postcards and brochures for you. All you really need is a mailing list.

Combine all of these ideas. Give them a phone call and then a week later, send a postcard. A few days later, stop

by with a brochure or flyer. Where most offline marketing wannabes make their mistake is simply giving up too soon. Most people will not hire you on the first contact. It might take five!

Market daily. You'll generally spend more time marketing

than actually 'working'. Doing the actual work for the clients is the easy part. Set a goal each day for what you want to accomplish.

You'll find that it takes about an hour to make 20-25 after-hours phone calls when you include the answering machine time. How many phone calls are you going to make each day?

If you go to strip malls, you can hand out a lot of flyers in an hour. Do you know where all of your local strip malls are located? Office parks can be another good location to get a lot done in a hurry.

Strive to send out some mail each day.

Have a spreadsheet to keep track of who you've contacted. Make a note of the date and the method. Don't beat a dead horse – five contacts and then they're out!

Utilize your friends and family. Posting a notice on your Facebook page might be all you need to find someone that knows of a good client. You might even find a good client among your friends and family.

All your message needs to say is, "Hey everybody, I'm starting an offline marketing business to help small business owners advertise their businesses effectively online. If you know of anyone that needs help in this area, please let me know. Thanks!"

Remember to include the contacts in your phone and email account(s). Send off a message to everyone you know and let them know that you're in business.

Ask for referrals. Small business owners tend to know other small business owners. Don't be afraid to ask for referrals when you're talking to them. This is especially true after you've done some work for them.

Expand your business. You can easily take on an unlimited number of clients and add more services if you outsource some of your tasks.

With outsourcing, you could just focus on your marketing and let others do the actual work of the services you're offering! Find others to do the work at places like fiverr.com and warriorforum.com.

You could even outsource a lot of your marketing. Simply pay a commission that still leaves you in profit for each sale. A lot of work-at-home telemarketers work on commission and could make many contacts for you in a short period of time.

Making $500 or more, quickly, is really quite simple. Get together some basic marketing materials and get them out there to as many suitable people as possible. In a good, solid day, you could make 100 phone calls, pass out 100 flyers, and contact everyone in your phone or email account.

The yellow pages and Val-Pak will keep you busy for a long, long time with a never-ending supply of potential clients.

If you'll limit your search to smaller companies that are already advertising, you're halfway home. The only other requirement is to never stop marketing. Hit each potential client five times.

If you stay busy and are aggressive in your efforts, $1,000 each week can be a realistic goal!

CHAPTER 14

HOW TO FIND A HIGHER PAYING JOB IN 60 DAYS

At one time or another, everyone has felt the need to find a new job. It's been said that you should start looking for a new job the first day you start a job. That might be a bit extreme, but the general sentiment is sound.

Staying with the same company has certain drawbacks. The opportunities are limited since someone else has to leave before you can move into a new position. You might not get along with your boss or co-workers. Being in one corporate environment can get stale. You're never going to get a big raise without a promotion. The list goes on.

Sometimes you just want to make more money. Regardless of your reasons for leaving, you can find a much better and higher paying job in 60 days. All it takes is persistence and regular activity.

Follow these strategies to land that perfect job in record time...

Develop a target. Rarely can you get a great job if you don't know what you're looking for. A good place to start is to make a list of all the things you like about your job that you still want in your new job. Then make a list of all of the things you don't like about your current job. Decide what you would change and add those positive items to your new job list.

For example, maybe your commute is too far. You might add an item that states, "Within 20 minute drive from home."

Be specific about what you want. Include the hours, the pay, what your co-workers and boss will be like, benefits and everything else that's important to you. Be clear about what you want.

Set your goal. You goal should read something like this:

"On or before (date 60 days from today), I will be employed in my perfect job which has the following characteristics:" Then list all the characteristics you developed from the previous step.

Reinforce your goal daily. Every morning and night you should read your goal aloud and imagine being employed in that perfect job. This will result in your unconscious really understanding what you want and make it a priority. Don't skip this step – it's far more important than you realize!

Brainstorm. Ask yourself, "What do I need to do to find this perfect job?" Listen to that little voice in your head and write everything down. In a typical brainstorming session, a lot of the ideas might be junk, but there's always some good stuff you can use.

Take action. Follow your list of actions. A little bit each day adds up over time. Use your evenings and weekends. Use your lunch break but be careful!

Market You!

Some people seem to think that just knowing what they want and visualizing it is enough to make it happen. Doubtful. But it is enough to allow you to spot opportunities that will help you become employed in that new job. Once your brain knows what you're looking for, it will spot opportunities all over the place.

When you find those opportunities, in order to secure your perfect job, you still must show the companies what you can do for them! This is part of marketing also; it's marketing you!

These strategies can turn you into a well-oiled marketing machine:

Tell everyone you know. Call everyone you can think of and let them know that you're looking for a new job. Tell your neighbors and the person on the next treadmill at the gym. Tell your family. Tell your mail carrier. Anyone not associated with your current job is fair game.

Contact your prospective employers. Call all the companies that might meet your criteria and ask for the person for whom you would likely work. If you're a production manager, ask for the plant manager. When you get them on the phone, tell them that you're looking for advice and ideas. Everyone likes to give advice.

Avoid asking for a job. They'll simply say that there's nothing available and the call will end. On the other hand, if you ask for advice and ideas, you'll start to develop a relationship. Over time, this can really pay-off.

Ask your friends if they know anyone that works at the company. You can also scan the company website. Find the person that you need to talk to; it helps to have a name. You can find a name if you're persistent.

If you can develop a relationship with this person, they will likely let you know if something becomes available or if they hear about any other opportunities.

Send a letter to the high-ranking person at that company. These are the people that have the power to do things that many hiring managers cannot do, like create positions. Tell them why you're interested in their company and what you can do for them. Make the letter relatively informal.

Good people are the hardest commodity to find. Convince this person that you're a good person and would make a good employee.

You might even tell them about your list of criteria for your job. Just having that list is more impressive than you realize.

Be creative. Have you ever had to look at 100 resumes to fill a position? It's mind numbing, at best. Everyone looks the same after a while. Anything that makes you standout (within reason) is a good thing.

There's a story of a guy that used Google Adwords to find a job. He bid on the names of hiring directors. Obviously, these are going to be cheap keywords.

He created an ad that said, "Googling yourself is fun. Hiring me is fun, too." He also included his phone number in the ad.

When these directors Googled themselves, they saw the ad and clicked on it. All but one of the directors called and interviewed him. He got a job at a total cost of $6.

What ideas can you come up with to stand out from the crowd in a positive way? If you look like everyone else, you're going to struggle.

Use social media. If you have a blog, Facebook page, Twitter account, Linked In profile, or anything similar, put it to good use. You might even consider offering a reward to anyone that lets you know of an opening that you ultimately get.

Even strangers on the street might help. You never know... that person at the bus stop or walking their dog at the park just might know of the perfect opportunity. If you're at a social gathering, let everyone know about your job search.

Don't stop. A little activity each day results in a lot of momentum. You've given yourself 60 days, so keep busy for 60 days. A job search is one of those situations that result in being told 'no' a lot. Keep going.

Improve your interview skills. Most people don't spend a lot of time interviewing, so most people don't get a lot of practice. A little bit of practice can quickly put you head and shoulders above the competition. Get a book about job interviews. Get a friend to interview you. Practice, practice, practice.

Finding a new job is a job in itself. Don't let it get you down. Keep focusing on how great it will be to have that ideal job and the bigger paycheck. When you get frustrated, always go back to that mental picture.

It's very difficult to fail at anything if you have a clear target that you reinforce daily, you take action every day, and you don't give up. Even if it's just dumb-luck, you're going to find something sooner or later that meets your criteria. The only way to fail is to settle for less.

Set a goal. Stay busy. Leverage every person and resource you can think of. You'll be employed in that great job soon!

CHAPTER 15

DRIVING FOR DOLLARS

Developing an alternative income stream that provides either a steady feed or occasional trickle of extra cash can make your life easier and even help you fund your retirement.

Have you ever considered driving for dollars? Interestingly, plenty of people with good driving skills are capitalizing on this skill to bring in some cash.

You can too!

These tips will help you bring in extra money by driving.

DELIVERY OF RENTAL CARS FROM ONE LOCATION TO ANOTHER

If you live in a state with consistent tourism as one of its industries, you'll be pleasantly surprised at the money you can make driving vehicles from one city to another. Oftentimes, rental cars must also be driven from one airport to the next.

Contact the car rental companies in your area to offer your help in relocating their cars when they need them moved from one city to another, or even to different lots in the same city.

The money you make from delivering rental cars can be quite lucrative!

RV COURIER WORK

You can also be paid to travel the countryside, driving an RV from one location to another. Furthermore, the company that hires you to move the RVs will cover costs of gasoline, insurance, and your fare to get back home. An additional amount will be added to your paycheck - about 25 to 35 cents per mile you drove in the RV.

What's nice about being an RV courier is you can do it on

the weekend. So, regardless of whether you're a college student, full-time worker, or retired, you can be an RV courier for a couple of days a week.

So if you've always wanted to see more of the sights in North America, you can actually be paid to do it!

Another benefit about being an RV courier is the company you drive for wants you to take your time and be a safe driver, so there's no real work stress. And usually, it doesn't require a commercial drivers' license to drive an RV.

What an incredible way to boost your income!

DELIVERY OF NEW COMMERCIAL VEHICLES TO BUYERS

Although you can also beef up your income by delivering new commercial vehicles from the manufacturers to those who ordered them, you may find it's necessary to have a commercial drivers' license to do it, depending on the size of the vehicle.

Interestingly, these jobs are available now and companies that manufacture rescue vehicles, school buses, and large utility trucks for municipalities are consistently taking applications for drivers to deliver these special-ordered vehicles.

AVAILABILITY OF DRIVING FOR DOLLARS JOBS

According to the popular driving for dollars website, Travel for Pay, approximately 5,000 new jobs are available each month in the driving industry.

When you see someone driving a utility truck, rescue vehicle, or school bus, you simply think they're going about their lives and doing their jobs in those industries. In fact, those drivers may be paid individuals who are delivering those vehicles to the proper owners.

Seasonal driving work during the spring and summer is especially plentiful as new school buses are often delivered before the new school year and vacationers are shopping for their new RVs during those seasons.

Teachers, in particular, appreciate the plentiful driving for dollars jobs available in May, June, and July as they can have as much work driving as they want while school is out.

REQUIREMENTS FOR DRIVING TO BOOST YOUR INCOME

Most companies who hire drivers to move their vehicles require drivers to be at least 18 years of age. You must also have a decent driving record with few traffic tickets and no serious accident history. Possession of a legal drivers' license is necessary.

If you live in a state that offers a Chauffeurs' license, you'll likely want to apply for and receive one before you begin your driving for dollars job with vehicles weighing 13 tons or less. But no worries, it is apparently a very simple test you can study for in 30 minutes or less at your local drivers' license facility. Then, go ahead and take the test that day while the knowledge is fresh.

In the event you plan to drive heavy vehicles weighing 25,000 pounds or more, you would likely want to apply for and obtain a commercial or Class B license. We're talking about driving semi-trucks and trailers or large utility trucks here. It's up to you to check out the available driving work in your state to determine whether you'd require this license.

The fact is most of the vehicles to be driven and delivered fall into the Class A (under 25,000 pounds), which means either your regular drivers' license or the Chauffeurs' license, if your state offers it, would be all that's necessary.

WHAT YOU MAKE DRIVING FOR DOLLARS

AND HOW YOU'LL BE PAID

If you do this type of driving full-time, some estimates of

pay, according to experts in the industry, top $200 per day you drive. As mentioned earlier, most companies will pay you 25 to 35 cents per mile driven, cover the cost of fuel, and the return trip home.

In some cases, the company will pay for a night in an inexpensive hotel if the trip requires it and if you're not driving a vehicle you can sleep in. Your meals, however, are on you and aren't paid for by the company you're driving for.

If you were to drive for dollars full-time, you could make between $50,000 and $60,000 yearly.

For most driving jobs, you'll be considered a self-employed contractor and will receive gross wages and sent a 1099 at the end of the year. You'll, therefore, be required to pay all your own taxes and report your wages to the IRS.

You'll be given the expense money for gas, nights in a hotel (if necessary), and your return trip up front. When you complete the work, you'll receive your pay per miles. There may be unique opportunities and ways you can get paid travelling in both directions, which means you'll really rack up the cash in a few days' time.

SIDE BENEFITS OF DRIVING FOR DOLLARS

The Obvious: You Get to See the Country

If there are a lot of places in North America you want to see, you'll finally get your chance to do so, free of charge. Most companies will approve taking a detour off the route to see something nearby, as long as you subtract those miles from the total miles they'll be paying you for.

Also, most of the companies will allow you days at the end of your driving trip to do whatever you wish. So if you're driving an RV to Seattle and your Aunt Tillie lives there, you'll be able to spend a few days with her after you deliver the RV.

You Can Travel with a Loved One or Two

Something that makes this type of work extra fun is you can take your partner or good friend along with you, if you wish. If both of you drive a vehicle after you reach the point of vehicle pick-up, you could make combined totals of $65,000 to $80,000 yearly, according to the Travel for Pay website.

You Might Build Up Huge Numbers of Frequent Flyer Miles

In the event you use your return travel dollars to fly home, you'll be gathering a decent amount of free miles, depending on how often you drive. Those miles are money-saving extra benefits as you and your loved ones could take some pretty nice trips in and out of the country.

SUMMARY

Driving for extra money can be some of the most fascinating work you'll ever do to boost your bottom line.

The potential to earn steady, large amounts of extra money

definitely exists. And with the numerous perks of the job, especially the incredible adventures and sight-seeing you'll experience, you'll see this job has many attractive benefits.

Go ahead, take over the wheel, and enjoy your trips!

CHAPTER 16

MAKE EXTRA MONEY BY CREATING VIDEOS

FOR SMALL BUSINESSES

Would you like to boost your income quickly and easily? If so, making YouTube videos to market small businesses is a great way to do it.

Many businesses are looking for ways to get into the digital age. In fact, you might not even have to make a true video. In most cases, a simple slideshow set to music is just as good, if not better.

Making these videos is a simple business that requires little to no skill except for some determination and a little creativity. Not only that, but many of the businesses will already have high quality photos that you can use.

GETTING STARTED

As with many businesses, it's all in the marketing. The hardest part will be finding clients, but it's not too difficult as long as you're willing to put in the time and effort.

There are many ways to find clients. Choose the method that appeals to you. Ideally, you would utilize all of the methods to ensure a steady stream of clients.

Consider these options for finding clients:

Cold calling is perhaps the most effective method.
There is no better way to find clients than simply picking up the phone and dialing. You can follow this script:

"Hi, my name is _____. I'm taking a video marketing class and I have to find a business to use for one of my projects. Are you the person to talk to about that?"

When you get the correct person on the phone: "I'm looking for a business to use for a class project. It entails making 2 videos and doing all the marketing to get a business to the top of the Google search results. The cost would be $175. Is that something that you would be interested in?"

Obviously, it will be dishonest to claim you are taking a

class if you're actually not. So find a free class online and sign up. You'll learn a lot and you can honestly claim to be taking a class. Many people love to help others that are learning.

You should expect to average a client every 20 calls or so, which should take about an hour.

Using this method allows you to call many more people in the same amount of time it takes to drive to a business. The phone also doesn't require the expense of gasoline.

Just show up at the business. You can use the same basic script, but go door-to-door and approach business owners. It usually takes less than 20 approaches to find a new client. So the numbers can be better than cold calling.

Advertise your service on Craigslist. The best category for your posting would probably be Computer > Gigs. Keep in mind that your post can only be renewed and moved back to the top of the list once every few days.

You may have to post more frequently than that. This means you'll require a few posts that are different enough that the filters won't realize what you're doing.

Ideally, you would want to post at least twice a day. Pick a time when people are likely to be online looking at posts.

Use e-mail. You can use a 'Craigslist e-mail scraper', which you can find online. There are free options, so consider taking advantage of them. **Use this tool to scrape the 'Jobs' category for email addresses.** Ignore the email addresses that have 'craigslist' as part of the address. Email the others with your offer.

Just send one email to each business. Avoid being a spammer!

Ideally, you'll want your own email address, which means getting your own web domain. You don't have to actually create a website, but having your own email address makes everything easier.

An email service like Yahoo or Gmail can work, but you'll be limited to a certain number of emails before they start putting limits on you.

Use the bcc: option and send a single email to hundreds of recipients at a time. You'll be sending out an average of about 400 emails before someone says yes.

Think about targeting the following types of businesses:

Furniture stores, bridal shops, boutiques, gift shops, dry cleaners, and carpet cleaning services. **The key is to stay away from the**

well-known business chains. For example, McDonald's won't be letting you do marketing for them.

Once you have a client, do some research:

Find keywords to use in marketing each client. The Google keyword tool at HYPERLINK "https://adwords.google.com/" https://adwords.google.com/ is a free tool you can use. There are other keyword tools as well. If you're familiar with another that you prefer, feel free to use it instead.

What you're looking for are appropriate search terms. **Ideally, you want search terms with high popularity, but relatively little competition.** The Google keyword tool will tell you, which terms are searched the most and how many people are buying advertising at Google for those terms.

For example, if you were working with a bridal shop in Boise, you might check on the terms boise wedding dress, boise bridal, boise bridal shop, boise wedding store, boise wedding accessories, boise wedding dress alterations, and so on.

Try using the local zip codes in place of the city name.

Take your results to the business owner and try to get a feel for what he or she thinks about marketing with those terms. For example, she might tell you that a certain search term is likely to be used by people that are just looking for information instead of looking to spend some money, so it would be a waste to use such terms.

MAKING THE VIDEOS

Now it's time to make your videos:

The first option is to make a real video. It's difficult and expensive to make a truly professional looking video, so just do your best. Instead, pull out your cell phone and make a testimonial video telling your audience what you like about the business.

Make a slideshow. Head over to the business and take about 50 pictures with your digital camera. Ask the owner what items sell the best and get some pictures of those.

You'll only use approximately 15-20 good pictures.

If you're lucky, the business will already have photos for you! These photos are likely to be high quality, too. Ask for them and use them in an interesting slide show.

Use Windows Movie Maker to create videos. This program is part of Microsoft Windows and it's very easy to use. There are other programs you can use that are similar. **With Movie Maker, you simply drag the photos into the program.** Keep these points in mind:

At the end of the video, put in a title slide that lists the name, address, contact information, and hours of the business you're promoting.

The video should be 45-60 seconds long.

Play around with the various effects in the movie-making program. A little movement can make your slideshow much more interesting.

Add in some music. There's free music available at HYPERLINK "http://incompetech.com/music/" http://incompetech.com/music/. Find something that sounds good and fits nicely with your video.

Upload your video to YouTube.com. Millions of people upload videos. Their website has easy-to-follow instructions.

The title of the first video should be in the format of Business Name | phone number | city name | zip code | keyword.

The title of the second video should be keyword #2 | phone number | city name | zip code | keyword #3.

Ping your videos. Go to HYPERLINK "http://www.Pingler.com" www.Pingler.com and let the search engines know that your videos exist. Your keywords will serve as the title and the URL will be the web address of your videos. Both videos will need to be pinged. The website is self-explanatory regarding how to do this.

GETTING PAID

Now show the business owner their new online videos at YouTube. It's practically unheard of for a business owner to be dissatisfied with the videos. But if there are any issues, do your best to resolve them immediately.

The only thing left to do now is get paid! Provide the business owner with a simple invoice. There are plenty of free invoice templates available online for use with any popular word processing program. Take your check to the bank and move on to the next client. It's really that simple.

ADDITIONAL POINTERS

It's much easier than you think to find clients. You'll need to stay on top of getting new clients. However, you shouldn't deal with any clients that are being unreasonable or non-cooperative.

Keep marketing. Your primary job is marketing and securing new clients. The rest of your business is fast and easy.

Consider marketing to clients that are out of town. If you live in a small community with limited commerce, you might want to branch out to a wider geographic area. If you work with out of town clients, just mention that they'll be supplying the photos.

Be clear about how much and when you'll be paid. It's important that everyone is on the same page. When talking to the business owner, say something like, "I'll make the videos, and you'll pay me after you have approved them. I want you to know that it may take a few weeks before we begin seeing results from this marketing campaign."

Be flexible. Think about the market in your local area. Maybe making one video for $100 will be more attractive to your potential clients.

Do as much as you can on the phone and online. It gets expensive and time consuming to drive all over the place. Use the phone and internet resources to help you get clients and keep in touch with them along the way.

Making videos for small businesses is an excellent way to make some extra money. It could even turn into your new career. This business is easy, fun, and helpful to the local business owners in your community.

CHAPTER 17

7 STEP TO AFFILIATE MARKETING PROFITS

Affiliate marketing is a lucrative and easy way to make money online. As an affiliate, you sell other people's products for a commission. So you don't have to create a product or offer customer support. Your only real job is to promote the product.

What's even better is that you can set up your business in a way that everything practically runs on autopilot. Once you set it up, you can make money for several months, or possibly even years, without touching the website again.

Following this 7-step process will quickly get you making money in affiliate marketing:

Choose your niche. This is certainly one of the most critical steps for success in affiliate marketing. If you choose a niche that's too large, there's likely to be too much competition for success to come easily. Choose a niche that's too small and you'll never have enough customers to be really profitable. Tips for choosing a niche:

Sell solutions. What is a common challenge that many people have that you know how to solve? If you're familiar with the dilemma, it will be easier to market products that offer a solution.

Cater to cherished hobbies. What topics are you knowledgeable about that many are fanatical about? Promote products related to popular hobbies and activities.

Meet an emotional need. What are people afraid of? Most of us are afraid of being alone, missing out on the good things in life, or not being successful. Sell a product that resolves those fears.

The three most successful niches tend to be love, money, and health. Narrow one of these broad topics down to a sub-topic. For example, in the love niche, sub-topics can include getting back your "ex," finding "the one," dating success, and many more. You can narrow it even further by catering to one gender.

Find your keywords. Spend some time researching good keywords in your niche. The Google Adwords Keyword Tool is one of the most popular methods of discovering popular keywords that people use when looking for information or products in your niche.

What you're looking for is a keyword related to your niche that is getting a significant number of searches, but for which there is not too much competition. The Google keyword tool is pretty self-explanatory when it comes to these numbers. A good minimum is 1,500 searches per month.

Your keywords will be the cornerstone of your marketing plans. All of your marketing efforts will revolve around these keywords.

Choose a product. There are several affiliate network sites, but Clickbank is certainly the largest. Also, take a look at Commission Junction. Obviously, you want to consider how much you will earn per sale, but that's not the only important detail.

Take a look at the sales page. How does it look to you? Does the sales page peak your interest and make you want to buy the product? If you wouldn't buy it, you shouldn't expect anyone else to either. Ensure the sales page looks professional

Does the product have a guarantee or a warranty? How good is it? Would you be wary of buying this product with the guarantee or warranty that is provided?

Perhaps most importantly: is this a product that people in your niche would be willing to spend money on?

Get a domain name. Your domain name also contributes to your sales success. This is the first place your keyword will come into play.

Include your keyword in your domain name. For example, if your keyword was "lose 30 pounds in 30 days," your domain name could be "lose30poundsin30days.com." It's very likely that the domain name you want won't be available, but there are ways around this issue.

For example, the domain name "lose30poundsin30daysnow.com" might work for you. Or perhaps, "lose30poundsin30dayseasily.com" would work well too. Just try to be sure that your keyword comes first in your domain name. Add anything extra at the end.

Most studies have shown that .com endings are best. Most top affiliate marketers avoid other suffixes, with the exceptions of .net and .org.

There are many places to register domain names. GoDaddy.com is the most popular.

Build a website. The easiest way to a full-blown website is

by using Wordpress software. You can get it free at wordpress.org and look over the tutorials about how to upload the software to your hosting. Many hosting companies also have "1-click" installation for Wordpress.

Post content on your site every day for the first couple of weeks, and then 2 or 3 times a week thereafter. This will keep your readers and the search engines coming back for more.

Put a newsletter sign-up form on your website and communicate with your subscribers regularly. Your subscribers are your list and your list is like gold. Cultivate a relationship with them and they'll buy from you time and time again. A popular autoresponder service is Aweber, and there are many more as well.

Create lots of backlinks. One way to make your website more relevant is to create a lot of backlinks. These are links that point back to your website. Search engines place a high value on these.

One good strategy to create backlinks and gain some readers is by writing articles and posting them at article directories. These articles will contain a short bio with a link to your website for promotion.

Other ways to create backlinks include posting on forums, posting on blogs, and registering your website with the numerous website directories. Don't forget to create a Facebook page and Twitter account. Utilize websites like Squidoo, as well.

Keep repeating the process. One website and one product to promote are unlikely to create a large amount of income. It will be necessary to promote several products, each with their own corresponding website. You can stay within the same niche or you can use a new niche each time.

Once you have a process that works for you, it becomes easy. Simply repeat the process over and over again. Keep in mind that some of your websites might fail to make money. But a few of your websites will make a lot of money. So it only makes sense to create multiple sites with multiple products.

As you can see, making money with affiliate marketing is not that difficult. It can be time-consuming, but it's also possible to outsource a lot of the work. Many successful affiliate marketers hire someone to build their websites. They also hire people to write their articles. The most important part of the process is finding profitable keywords and products.

Always ensure you are in a niche that appeals to have a sufficient number of customers. Remember that someone has to actually buy the product for you to make any money.

Take note of what works for you and what does not. This process lends itself to constant improvement. Don't wait!

The sooner you start, the sooner you'll see some profits.

ABOUT THE AUTHOR

Paul Coan, CFP®, ChFC®, CEA®

Several publications have identified Paul Coan as standing out as a wealth manager such as Consumer's Research Council naming Paul as one of America's Top Financial Planners for eight years running. Worth Magazine named him one of the Top 250 Wealth Advisors. Bloomberg's Wealth Manager has listed him in their annual Top Dog Report on numerous occasions.

Paul is a CERTIFIED FINANCIAL PLANNER™ professional which is the most recognized financial planning designation in the world. He also holds a Chartered Financial Consultant (ChFC®) designation, the most extensive education available for professionals seeking a designation in financial planning. As a Certified Estate Advisor (CEA®) and a member of the National Association of Financial and Estate Planning, Paul has broad knowledge of estate planning and asset protection strategies. He is also a Registered Financial Advisor with the National Association of Personal Financial Advisors(NAPFA). NAPFA is the nations leading organization dedicated to the advancement of Fee-Only compensation and fiduciary standards.

Paul lives in Indiana with his wife Ann and their son.

www.ingramcontent.com/pod-product-compliance
Lightning Source LLC
Chambersburg PA
CBHW051701170526
45167CB00002B/491